T0105499

Mothering Mother

A Daughter's Experience in Caregiving

by Martha Cooper Eischen

iUniverse, Inc.
Bloomington

Mothering Mother
A Daughter's Experience in Caregiving

The information, ideas, and suggestions in this book are not intended as a substitute for professional medical advice. Before following any suggestions contained in this book, you should consult your personal physician. Neither the author nor the publisher shall be liable or responsible for any loss or damage allegedly arising as a consequence of your use or application of any information or suggestions in this book.

iUniverse books may be ordered through booksellers or by contacting:

iUniverse
1663 Liberty Drive
Bloomington, IN 47403
www.iuniverse.com
1-800-Authors (1-800-288-4677)

Because of the dynamic nature of the Internet, any Web addresses or links contained in this book may have changed since publication and may no longer be valid. The views expressed in this work are solely those of the author and do not necessarily reflect the views of the publisher, and the publisher hereby disclaims any responsibility for them.

ISBN: 978-1-4502-7352-7 (sc)
ISBN: 978-1-4502-7354-1 (ebk)

Library of Congress Control Number: 2010917275

Printed in the United States of America

iUniverse rev. date: 12/06/2010

To

Mother Love

My inspiration, encouragement, and strength, whose care was my privilege and joy, who gave her indomitable spirit and heavenly smile to the world, who upon her retirement, was given a beautiful gold pin, on which was inscribed:

"à notre rose unique au monde" – to our rose unique in all the world!

Table of Contents

Acknowledgements

It would be impossible to name all those who deserve my special thanks for helping me to help Mother Love live life to its fullest during her twilight years. To those nameless, I pour out my deepest gratitude. To the others, whose names remain fresh in my heart, I especially mention here:

My Family:

- Brother Paul and wife, Terry, always an unquestioning rock of support and love.
- Sister Mary and husband Al Malischewski, unconditionally available, no call too late, no task too great. They were always "there" with extraordinary devotion and love. The title of this work was Mary's inspiration!
- Brothers David and wife, Gay; Stephen; Andrew and wife, Mary Ann, who from afar lent uplifting love, encouragement and cheer in ways too numerous to mention.

Caregivers:

- Callie Brown – who shared the precious journey with us, not just as caregiver extraordinaire, but truly another daughter to Mother Love. Any "thank you" is inadequate.
- The staff of the Main Line Adult Day Center, whose 5 years of loving care made the center her "home" by day.

Personal Physician:

- James Morris, MD, Main Line Health, our family physician - a real partner to me, on whose practical wisdom and advice I depended.

Kind and Generous Testimonials:

- Charles L. Cooper, PhD, CEO, Human Resource Consultants, PA, Mental Health Group Practice, Central North Carolina
- William W. Lander, MD, Family Physician
- Kent Bream, MD, University of Pennsylvania, Director Sayre Health Center
- Stephanie J. Yocum, Past Director, Main Line Adult Day Center
- The Rev. Michael Pearson, Rector, St. Mary's Episcopal Church, Wayne, PA
- Ruth L. Mooney, PhD, MN, Nursing Research Facilitator, ChristianaCare Health System
- Hermine Isaak, Lupus Foundation
- Dorianne N. O'Hara, R.N. (Retired) Critical Care Clinician

Reviewing of this work:

- William and Rebecca Creese
- Mary E. Hamilton

Idea:

- The Scriptorium, All Saints Convent, Catonsville MD – for capturing the essence of my message in a single phrase (See Rose Photo Back Cover)

Introduction

I was never a mother. Today I am. I never had parenting skills. Now I have them. Everything I learned about caregiving, I learned in the last seven years, and I am now of retirement age! This book is dedicated to all the caregivers and their loved ones who are journeying now, or will be, down the road to the end of the rainbow. Though it is written from the perspective of the care of a mother, I mean to embrace both men and women. For, it is the men and women of our lives, entering their twilight years, and we, the men and women who care for them, who are the subject and concern of this book.

Books and pamphlets on the subject of caregiving, take many different perspectives. There are clinical, pastoral, practical, and perhaps many other approaches to this monumental task. The job really encompasses them all. I hope that this little book will feed the caregiver or caregiver-to-be the nourishment from all those perspectives, and be a kind of well, from which to draw much comfort, love, and support, along with helpful ideas for daily use.

Fortunately, we are often given plenty of time to grow into the job. Our fears, mistakes, anger, frustration, joys, gratitude, love, and the ultimate of stress are wrapped up in the new and immense chore in front of us - caring for our loved one, often our parent, as the days wane in that treasured life. It is a privilege and a joy to be called to do this work. It is transforming. Although we are doing so much giving, so is our loved one. We trudge along, not knowing how long the road is, how bumpy it will be, or how many turns we will have to make just to stay on the target. As we know, the target is to bring her safely through the twilight years of life, bolstered by the comforts of home and all that that means to a now very vulnerable human being.

We try to fill her life with love, warmth and security, in what has likely become the ultimate insecurity for her – old age, with all its relentless stripping away of life as she once knew it. She is old and fading. She is likely *more scared* than she can tell you. She knows where she has been and, probably has some idea where she is going. Thus, little by little, she has reason to be afraid as she loses her grip of just about everything she ever was or had. Fortunately for her as well, it comes slowly, by and large. Little by little, she is asked to let go of things she has always done or cherished, habits she has always kept, disciplines that have been her mainstay, and finally her health, physical and often mental. Her surrender is downright frightening. And all the while we think she should have *nothing* to worry about, because we are taking care of *everything!* What a journey this is. She needs our security, and we need her patience, wisdom, and willingness. We need each other. This is a journey in growth that will probably never happen again. Even if you are a healthcare professional, this task is different. This task changes us forever. It's a blessing to be embraced, even through, and perhaps especially in our tears.

Mother is a cum laude graduate of Bryn Mawr College, and also studied at the Sorbonne in Paris. She still speaks French fluently. She raised a family of six children, has fourteen grand-children, and at last count, has thirty-three great grandchildren. With all that responsibility, she gave mightily to her community as a volunteer most of her life. Almost all our growing- up days, she kept an elderly or indigent person in our home. She taught French, mostly but not exclusively, in high school. Finally, and most importantly, with my father she worshipped God in His church every Sunday, giving more than her tithe of time, talent and money to that work. How could one person have done so much? She did. She is one of the most powerful people I've ever known – mentally, emotionally, physically, and especially spiritually. If you meet one such person in your lifetime, you are indeed blessed. And, she's my mother! If you looked into her grace-filled face, you would know all that I cannot possibly tell you in the written word.

Seven years ago Mother suffered a tragic accident that left her with third degree burns over twenty-five percent of her body. She was hospitalized for five months, the first ten weeks of which she was unconscious. She turned eighty-eight while in her coma. Miraculously she recovered, underwent rigorous rehabilitation, returned to a relatively independent life, and continued a daily routine that touched many lives. Although this period was the beginning of decline, she kept a very active and involved life to the degree that she could handle. Only two strokes, which she suffered five years later, shut down her independence and made her daily routine include day care and structured supervision.

Today she is my child. Oh, she knows what's going on, all right. She's just the same person she always was, only now she is returned to dependence. A new dimension for her and me! Now she has virtually no memory. But, she still has her brain. She still thinks pretty clearly for someone whose vision is reduced to NOW – no five minutes ago, and no forward glance – just now. What's going on, *now*? But, unlike the child who never knew anything, she has known it all – and *done* it all! Now, she has to learn to let go of it all, keep her dignity, follow directions even when she doesn't want to, and, depend on someone else to make it through a day. There's a lot of fear in this, a testing of whether she can trust you, or whoever is in charge of her at the moment. The aging adult has a lifetime of experience to look back on – even though through dim lenses. Can we help in that backward glance? Can we make it a fond memory, or if not a memory, a fond feeling, filled with love and security? The last five minutes, the last episode, filled with the only thing that counts – love.

I hope this little book may be a very big encouragement to any caregiver just stepping onto this winding path – or to anyone, for that matter, who may have been following it for some time now. Come with me as I share my life with Mother Love, the tender name I call her and everyone else calls her who journeys with her daily.

1943

Mother Love and Her Children

2005

1. The Certainty of Decline

Just as no parent is prepared for the first child, so neither is the caregiver prepared for the duty of caring for a declining loved one. No matter what you read or hear, or whom you know who's been there before you, you likely can't be prepared for this task. You will often feel uncertain, unprepared, inadequate, and unfit. It's OK! You just go on. Trip over your mistakes, and feelings, and just go on. This duty is underscored by love and has a loving Teacher.

None of us is fully prepared to believe that our loved one is slipping, especially slipping enough to be scary. But, no matter how smart she is, she *is* slipping. The first incident that concerned me was before mother had suffered any catastrophic events. I had sent her to the bank to make a deposit in my account. She simply forgot what my errand was about. So, she took the check and put it in *her* account. When I asked her about the deposit, she said she couldn't remember what I wanted her to do, so she put it in her own account. That's even after I had given her a deposit slip! That sort of incident may seem small to some folks, but it was a huge flag to me, for mother was simply too big a powerhouse to have made such a mistake, even at eighty-seven years of age. So, the evidence was clear *before* the adverse winds began to blow in her face. It can take months or years to develop symptoms, and so it can be equally as long, or longer, to get beyond the denial that those symptoms even exist. First you are shocked at some of them - simple things, reversions to childish likes and dislikes, changes in taste. It often starts with food preferences. (And this from a mother who would *never* have exhibited any inclination other than to finish the half-eaten leftovers from her children's plates, so as not to waste an ounce of food!) They are only the beginning. And they may last for years before any other symptoms appear.

So, life is changing – forever, not all at once, and not without many upswings. But the general trend is down, not up. My nephew, who is a physician, said rather casually, "It doesn't get better." What a light bulb of wisdom! If you can absorb that for all it says, you will be way ahead of the game. It was not meant to be a discouragement. It was meant to help. He considered it an honor to care for his ailing grandfather. I consider it the same, and more, as I care for Mother Love. I am encouraged and strengthened by that simple statement, as I face each new circumstance. There is a clear difference between training children and your declining loved one. When you are training children to stand up straight, or walk, or helping them to remember some event or person, unless they are impaired in some way, they *will* "get it" and go on to the next level of learning. Your loved one is declining. So she may or may not get it at that moment, and most likely, at some point, will not remember the next time. So for you, it will be a matter of progressive reinforcement. Some days will be better than others. The more rest she has, the more alert she will be, and then the better her retention and response.

Beyond the denial, there is finally acceptance. And this cycle will go on, for each thing that happens. There will be denial - an attempt to get beyond the new event, an attempt to get rid of it, or straighten it out, or correct the problem. That's not all bad. I try to challenge mother, at every turn, to achieve or perform as she has in the past, *recognizing that the time may be here when that particular thing is no longer going to happen as it did in the past* - the acceptance.

And so it will go, for every thing she does or slips from doing - denial, acceptance. Once you get used to the big changes, and accept them, it does get easier. One element of the denial, which makes it hard to let go of, is that there is a measure of shame that attaches to the acknowledgement. "I can't believe that *my* mother is doing that." The connotation is that it is OK that *your* mother may be in that place in her life, but not *my* mother! You start out answering for her, explaining for her, covering for her, correcting her. All this will fade slowly. She is where she is, and you need to accept it, loving her through it. What you *do* want to do is protect her dignity! That's not the same thing as protecting *your* dignity. She needs your undying support and protection. You can appropriately cover for her and shore her up in many ways that no one else will recognize. One simple example is recognizing people. It is very easy to say, as the person approaches, "Oh Mother, here comes Greg" or "Mother, you remember Greg," giving her the chance to pick right up and say, "Of course", not skipping a beat, and not needing to be embarrassed for a second. That's love in action!

This subject of facing the reality of decline is packaged in our own fears and other untapped emotions. So, for your own sanity and each other's peace, it is wise to assume that no upturn is permanent, but downturns may be. Hence, I reward her with encouragement when the good things happen. She needs the pat on the back.

This is a particularly vulnerable time. It is easy for her to feel abandoned, to have some sense of, "I'm no use anymore," or "I don't want to be any trouble." Even if she can't articulate it, fear, panic, and frustration are not uncommon.

Understanding this notion of decline helps prevent me from making unrealistic demands on her. It keeps my expectations realistic, preventing immense anxiety, which would affect *my* performance. I need to be "up" as much as possible – mentally, emotionally and physically.

Allow your understanding of the certain decline to be your strength. Keeping it in focus will keep you in reality.

This is a roller coaster ride. So, strap yourself in, say your prayers a lot, listen to others, read the pamphlet pearls which I resisted, and face each day with the best you have to offer. That's all you need. As my mother still says, "Just take what comes to hand." Simple, sage advice, from a tower of love! Each day, a new beginning and just one day at a time!

Dealing with Dementia

All the charts in the world, illustrating the brain before and after such events as stroke or Alzheimer's, cannot prepare you for the journey with the demon, dementia. There simply are certain facts about the loss that can only be explained in laymen's terms, by those who have experienced them.

A little diversion for a moment may help to fashion a picture of the mind. While very simplistic in its explanation, it helps to understand. In today's technological age, we can liken the brain to a computer, which was indeed designed to emulate it. RAM, or memory, is the short term work space where you process all the things you are doing right now, for instance reading e-mail, writing a letter, getting on the Internet. Whatever you are doing *right now*, is being processed in RAM. The second kind of "space" is called storage, or disk space. It is here that all the history of what you work on in RAM is kept: the last spread sheet you used, your bank records, or your family photo album from the last vacation, etc. Whenever you want to see the pictures from the trip, you simply call up the saved images and view them on your screen. Presto! The brain is much the same. It keeps things stored from the beginning of its life. Then those things are recalled frequently throughout life, as they are needed. When you recall things from your past – one minute ago, or fifty years ago, there can be a short circuit between the memory that thinks cognitively about what's going on here and now, and what is being brought back from "storage". That short circuit can cut off everything, or things from recent experience, like the last phone call, or conversation. The inability to recall recent events is called "short term memory loss". "Long term memory loss" is the inability to recall things in the distant past, birthdays, historical events in your lifetime, familiar faces, friends or family.

The degree to which your loved one suffers from these losses is best measured by your own experience. No magic test can prove what you know already from your regular observation and interaction. It is variable and ever-changing within the individual, and frequently from day to day. "Everything changes. Every day it's different," a fellow caregiver said in dismay, one day. That is often true, especially in the beginning.

Some folks say, "I don't know whether I would rather have physical or mental impairment." But I can say that the challenges of coping with caring for a person suffering from dementia are enormous. They are as much emotional as physical. The caregiver probably suffers more anxiety and stress with dementia caregiving than with any other. The need to "straighten out" her thinking is perhaps the biggest hurdle between you and your sanity. You want to clear up the confusion. Let her know she's not in Ohio, where she grew up; or that she is in her own home as she speaks; or that her father has been dead for forty years, etc., etc! It is so hard to accept that no matter how much we explain, they simply can't understand, or at minimum, won't remember in two minutes from now. If they could, they would react accordingly, gladly. They do not know! Your being reduced to frustration, guilt, and dreadful fatigue just puts you down on the bottom of your barrel – very alone. You must be prepared for this, so that the feelings do not become ghosts, which regularly haunt you.

The descent into mental impairment is tragic for everyone. But it seems especially challenging when it involves one's spouse or someone who has been an intellectual giant and powerful contributor all her life long. Such is the case of my mother. The trap to try to get her to understand just looms overhead like a cloud all the time. In some cases, as is also the case with my mother, she knows she doesn't "get it". So for her it is also a constant struggle to keep in touch with what is really true. That struggle alone produces in *her* a fear far beyond mine, and one she cannot express. I simply see it in her eyes and sometimes in her mood.

Think how it must feel to spend all your energy just trying to keep things straight, sorting out where you are, who's who, what's what. Mother spends virtually all her time sorting out her life "in the moment", and what's happening around her. Sometimes the goings-on around her are far too much for her to keep straight. So the din just leaves her tuning out or, less frequently, getting irritated. Much of the time, she just wants to retreat to a place where she feels safe. That means being in familiar surroundings, with familiar people, doing familiar, routine things.

The more you can keep things the same the happier she is, and therefore, you are happy as well. You find that your peace and happiness are based on hers. If she is at peace and cheerful, so are you. So, with that in mind, I seek to find those things and circumstances that comfort and encourage her.

Of all the afflictions besetting the elderly, this demon, for me, produces the most stress. The roller coaster ride is relentless. You just get your steam back, when something else shoots you down. Often perfectly healthy physically, the mentally impaired, little by little, are unable to do some of the simplest, or most basic tasks. Feeding herself is a good example. One day she can sit in front of her food and not have a clue that she is supposed to pick up the fork and start eating. Then another day she will do it unprompted! This is not something that will get better. Be prepared that it is likely *not* just a case of some imbalance that you or your physician can "fix", and then all will be back to normal again. It is a part of the roller coaster ride, and you just accept each day with its limitations and surprise performances. Always encourage the performances, but accept the shortfalls, because it *will* continue, up and down.

Tricky Things – In Dementia

Repetitive questions, one of the biggest challenges, are a direct result of memory loss. At first, the repeated questions are not too terrible. You can tolerate them, and engage her in other thoughts. But the incessant ones are the challenge.

When the going gets tough, and she seems to be on a broken record, I try some tricks, like the following:

- Change the subject

- Get another loved one on the phone just to chat. I call my sister or brother and just let her chat a bit, briefly, and then go on with what we are doing.
- Suddenly do something else. The suddenness breaks the rut.
- If all else fails, leave the room for a short spell.

Sometimes it is best to just go along with it. If she is fantasizing, go with it. One night she told me, with the sweetest smile, that she and my father, now dead eight years, had just been called to be the king and queen of Siam! Well, I can tell you, I got a star for my performance that night! I congratulated her and asked her if she was going to accept it, because it was a very hard job. She thought about that, and replied that she thought it would be best if she declined. That closed the subject sweetly, and off to bed we went. However, sometimes you feel constrained to straighten it out. This may or may not work. If it doesn't, drop it. It will go nowhere and drive you crazy. Try one of the tricks above. It will go away eventually. You just have to have several tricks up your sleeve, so *you* can live through it! This is without a doubt one of the most troublesome things to deal with. It'll fray your nerves faster than anything.

No matter what, however, I always speak normally to her, normal conversation. It is important to respect her ability to understand and respond. And, if she sometimes doesn't, I don't get upset. Pearls of wisdom still roll off her lips. I'm always learning about gentleness, kindness, and love from her at the most unexpected times. She is full of grace. She really does take everything, for the most part, as it comes. Therefore I honor her and talk sensibly to her. I don't pass her off as if her questions are irrelevant or out of order, even when they are! I expect the best, even though I know that a lesser response is realistic. I am always happily surprised when she has a very 'together' response to some situation or conversation. What a present joy! I take it for what it is worth – just that – a very present joy!

Surround Her with Love

Sister to Sister,
Heart to Heart

Love binds Sisters-in-law

Sharing with Friends

Mother Love
Enjoys her 32nd
Great Grandchild

Personality Changes

Sometimes your loved one seems to react totally differently than you would ever expect. Be prepared. There just are things about her that you never knew. Maybe her entire adult life she never displayed those personality quirks that she is now uninhibited enough to express, like being feisty or cranky when tired, as all of us can be! But she never was her entire mothering life, you say!! Sometimes the changes are brief. She's tired, hungry, *needs to go to the bathroom!* Any number of things is possible. I try to be sensitive enough to catch a pattern. Chances are they will happen again under the same set of circumstances. Just like a parent, I have come to be sensitive to the unique reactions that are hers under the circumstances.

Accepting the Change

Just accept her. It's hard to believe that our sweet mother could be irritable or fussy. Well, she can! Changes are sometimes catastrophic to us emotionally. If we are going to be prepared for anything, it is best for us to recognize this fact in ourselves, as well as in our loved one.

It is a good thing to take a sneak peek at your loved one when she doesn't know you are there. Does she have a scowl on her face? Is she feisty? Is she looking confused? You can't believe your eyes. Could that really be mother? It is. She needs your tenderness and encouragement every minute that you can give it, so she feels safe, free and happy with her current circumstance. After all, that is all she has, the present moment. Can you make it a good moment, to the best of your ability? No heroics are needed, just love and trying.

What about personality changes that don't go away? Do they need medication? A common one is edginess, especially at night. Now she can't sleep. Worse, now *you* can't sleep! Daily activity plays an important role. If she is kept busy all day, she's likely to sleep better at night! A cup of soothing tea, and a restful, relaxing environment just before bed can set the sleepy-time mood. If these should fail, there are mild medications that can solve the problem without threat of addiction or other unpleasant side effects. Ask your physician. There are natural solutions. Consult a health foods store. Nearly always, there's a solution that fits your concern. But you may have to experiment until you find the right fit.

Things she no longer can/will do

She begins to stop doing things. This scary phenomenon is inevitable. You will resist it every step of the way. And well you should. You should gently push your loved one to her limit. Here, *challenge* is the operative word. Not coercion, but challenge. Always push her to her limits. She will do her best if you ask it of her properly. But, surrender must always be right behind.

I find *myself* challenged between pushing to keep her doing what she has always done, and letting go because she cannot do it any longer. The thing I don't want to do I may very well be doing, which is transferring my anxiety onto her. I want her to *do it*. My own anxiety is very wrapped up in her ability to continue to perform. She can't – maybe! If she can't, and I try to make her, I will fill her with the very thing I am trying to prevent – a sense of inadequacy! She will retreat, not rise to the challenge the way I think she should. *We think pushing her to continue to do what she has always done will somehow help her to keep it together.* That is true to a certain degree.

But it will have just the opposite effect if she is pushed beyond her limit. That is the key. Up to that point, it is good. But beyond that, it is harmful. If my demands are out of line with her new level of performance, she'll simply bail out, fold, shutdown. I constantly try to understand her limits, so I can reinforce, not tear down her sense of doing well. We have to know when to let go, or as the old country song says, we must "know when to fold".

So, we need to be sensitive to our loved one's fear of failure, as well as *our* fear that she *will* fail. Same fear, different reasons. We must begin to accept the decline and all that goes with it, including our own surrender. Everyone will have more peace, and she will actually last longer. This is just the opposite from our gut reaction, which wants us to push forward like a fire brigade.

There will be a time, *slowly but surely*, when your loved one will stop doing something, which you will pick up. Personal hygiene is one of the hardest things to pick up. It's so personal. It's just hard to accept. I couldn't imagine brushing my mother's teeth, wiping her bottom, feeding her. I remember one time saying to her impatiently, "Mother, I'm not going to feed you." I do it all gladly now. Some things are easier than others. But, you don't surrender until it becomes necessary. That is not because you are stubborn, or don't want to take it on, but because it is something that you want her to continue to do, as long as she has any ability whatsoever. It keeps her "engaged". That is another key word – *engaged*. You want your loved one to be engaged as much as possible every day, at the level that she is capable of handling. Letting go is going to happen. That is the business you are in. But the "when" and "where" of it are so variable. The quality of the life that she has will be directly dependent on your ability to keep her engaged at her proper level.

Sometimes sweetening up the chore for her works – a teaspoon of honey helps the medicine go down. At the other end of getting ready for bed is getting *in* bed. After the teaspoon of pill-laced yogurt, there is the delicious egg custard waiting. Just like children, we all need to think there is something better at the other end*!* *Encouragement is the teaspoon of honey that helps the medicine of aging go down.*

Encouraging her, supporting her, embracing her, praising her - these are all what she once did for me (and still does, in so many ways). Now I do it for her.

So, although she may not perform a task as easily as she once did, I let her continue, until it is clear that I should simply take it over. After a while there is an acceptance, not weary resignation or "giving up", but simply an acceptance of things as they are. That gets easier. There are many things along the way that are frustrating. So, it is good to learn acceptance. Again, as Mother has often said to me, "Just take things as they come". Now, I'm learning just that.

Making Mistakes

If you thought you had it right, get ready for humility! You will make many mistakes. Take them in stride. Even for Ziggy, that everyday cartoon character, the simple steps worked. One of his daily cartoons read: "Things to do today: Pick yourself up. Dust yourself off. Start all over again." Ask for forgiveness quickly. You'll get it, with a measure of sweetness you never expected.

We are fragile!! A beloved friend who has a frail husband called me frantically. She just wanted a few minutes to share her latest "episode." She was beating herself up for doing and feeling all the "wrong" things. Her husband had just fallen, while 30 seconds out of her sight. In his fall, he took down a rather expensive little table, which smashed to smithereens! He was OK, just shook up! Table gone, and wife a basket case! Sound familiar? She was so remorseful for having thought about the loss of the table and having been upset with her husband for falling! I said, "Panic and anger, Huh?" She, somewhat relieved, said, "Yes, I guess you know!" "Know," I chuckled! I could have written the script. Moral to the story: forget the table. It's worthless in comparison to your loved one. Make your husband walk with a walker, *always (that's the new rule) whenever he is alone!* Closed case, happy ending!

Sharing with Others

The second moral to the story above is: you must have someone to talk to, notably someone close to you, friend or family – just to air your thoughts, think out loud. Sharing with others how we feel is extraordinarily helpful. Situations aren't half so formidable if you can share them and your options with someone who knows the "turf" and knows and cares about you.

It's just so hard to accept this onset of decline, and all the things that go with it day to day, without having someone who loves us and cares about us to share it.

"She was totally nuts last night, and drove me nuts, too." Being able to say that with love and reverence for who she is and the profound depth of her struggle is very important. *No guilty feelings!* Just share it with a loved one. It's purging, freeing. It allows humor to set in where despair and fatigue often seem to rule.

Engaging Her Meaningfully

Keeping Up Her
Skills Every Day

Son, Stephen Shares
a Hearty Laugh

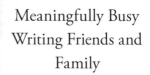

Meaningfully Busy
Writing Friends and
Family

Like Mother Like Son,
Paul Always Teaching

2. Engaging her

K eep her *engaged*! This is about maintaining the quality of her life – every day. One day off, and it can be two days backwards! So, I do as much as I can to keep her active and alert at her level of ability. I don't always know what that is. It changes. It goes up and down. But whatever it is, I make it my business to know it as best I can, and challenge her to be at that level until I see it change. Basically I am always, in some way or another, testing this degree. Even simple observations, throughout the day, are part of my daily lab work. Some days are better than others.

It is wise to be reminded that life for your loved one is now a series of challenges, *every day*. She truly needs to be stimulated to the degree she can handle. It affects her in every way - mentally, physically, and emotionally. This is where *she* passes or fails, with each little task. It is a chore. I just try to do my best one step at a time – each day.

One way of keeping her engaged is remembering family and friends' anniversaries, birthdays, special occasions, particularly those of grandchildren. It's a wonderful lift, not only for her, but for the one being remembered. Staying in touch keeps her engaged, especially with those she knows and loves. Whatever level she can handle, help her to do it.

Mother was a prolific writer. She never missed the occasions of her family and friends with cards of love. So when she was still able to write, but was already suffering from memory loss, I put sticky notes on each card, reminding her to whom she was writing, what for, and her relationship to them – Grandmother, Aunt, Godmother, Friend, and how she signed her name.

Another important thing is exercise and hobbies. Mother was a gifted pianist and organist in her time. So, I made sure that her routine included playing every day. It kept her engaged for an hour, mentally and physically. She continued that practice until her strokes took away that gift.

When she was able, she walked, with her walker, out to the mailbox, every day, and brought in the mail. It was an important part of her routine. As long as she can, I keep her engaged routinely, at her own level and pace.

Her ability to participate in various activities has changed, but it is critical to her well-being that she finds those things that keep her happily involved. I make a point of trying things out, some new, some old.

Surround Her with the Familiar

Several years ago, when mother was ninety-one, four of her six children took her to visit her many beloved friends in France. It was such a special, once-in-a-lifetime trip, with so many treasured memories and pictures. However, just two years later, after her two strokes, she was still physically quite capable of going away, so I decided to take her to the Jersey shore. It was close enough to home, in case she should suddenly need medical care. Three days into *that* vacation, we came home. It was too confusing. She couldn't keep it together. Home and the familiar made a great vacation, especially for me! The peace was a vacation!

Take Her Wherever She Can Go

Avignon, France –
Reliving a Memory

At 91, Sailing Down the
Seine with 4 of Her Children

Revisiting Alma Mater
in Paris

Fun at the Beach –
Wheelchair and All!

Stephen Takes Her for a Spin
Around Mt McKinley

So, taking trips, which thrilled her in the past, is no longer attractive. The known is safe, even if she forgets it every day. If you are able to say, lovingly, of course, "We do this everyday". Or, "This is your home. We're here every day." That's safe. *Sameness is not boring. It is safe!* Change is unsafe. It's frightening. The turf is unknown and therefore scary. Visit the same places, see the same movies, go for a drive in the same neighborhood. The sameness is reinforcing. It is encouraging because she remembers quickly by reminder. It's delightfully familiar. She'll love it just as much each time, as if it were the first time. It brings back good feelings and fresh memories.

Surround her, as well as yourself, with wonderful photo reminders of happy times, people, places, and events. A special one, perhaps one of her and you, can be placed many times throughout the house. I keep a special picture of Mother and Father, on their 60th wedding anniversary, in *each* room right where she sits, and by her bed. It's a picture that makes her happy and brings a beam across her face. When she forgets that she is home, I remind her that the picture of her and Father would only be in her home. It usually settles the matter quickly.

Habits and Routine

Perhaps nothing in life saves us more than our good habits. This truth is important, especially now. As our loved-one's memory fades, she needs to know and do things by rote. From the living room to the bathroom, we walk down the same hallway, pass the same pictures, and I give the same directions. Before I give the direction to turn to the right, she is already doing it, waiting for my affirmation. Everything that can be made into a good habit, I try to do. It not only saves time. It saves nerves – mine and hers.

Routine is very much in this same vein. I get more done when I can establish a routine that will carry us through when we're half awake. Out of the deep pockets of her brain, she does her routine nearly flawlessly. All she needs is encouragement, and, perhaps a helping hand. That's a lot different from maximum support. The discipline is not for discipline's sake, but for practicality's sake. Things get done with minimal disruption and confusion. When friends, family, or other helpers come to lend a hand, all routines are carefully written down. Nothing changes from her routine. Everyone is happy - helpers, too!

Challenge versus Coercion

There is a delicate balance between challenging and coercing, as I mentioned in "Things she no longer can/will do". Once a therapist, who was responsible for Mother's recovery from her tragic burn accident said to me, "I don't believe in coercion." I replied, "Neither do I, but I believe in challenging." You certainly don't want to force someone (actually you can't! They have many ways of refusing – acting like a donkey, playing possum!), but you do want to be creative about getting the job done. You do have a goal - eating dinner, walking to the toilet, brushing teeth, putting on a sweater, etc., etc. Ideally, and practically, you want to accomplish every task.

One morning I was not so successful. We were walking from the bedroom to the living room, and she got it into her mind that she couldn't make it. Plain and simple! So, she started to do all the wrong things – hunched back, bent knees, a few "I can'ts". I reacted just as badly. I barked directions - "stand up straight", "straighten your knees" - all to no avail. She was going to sit on the floor no matter what. So, losing the battle, I carefully let her sit on the floor. I called my good, care-giving neighbor who came immediately. In one quick lift, seconds later, mother was walking sweetly, with the two of us, one on each arm, to her chair, not remembering what just happened!

Each incident teaches me something, especially about myself! I learned to be creative. I use humor, pleading, logic, distraction, tenderness, just about everything my creative juices can muster. But the key is getting her to *will* to do what needs to be done. Resistance is a matter of the will. So, no matter how small the issue is, I try to get her to *will* to cooperate. Give me your hand; bend your knee; put on your glove; open your mouth. Sometimes it's a challenge, especially when eating!! But other times, we just need to remind ourselves that the trick is the will.

There are very tender moments in the midst of otherwise tense times. We are trying to reach our goals, while realizing that the very moment we're in may be the last. Thus, it is that very moment that becomes the goal. Cherish the moment!

Again, during the recovery from her burns, she tried to write. So, we gave her writing paper and a pen, and away she went. Those precious letters were illegible! But they were her struggle and final victory over her infirmity. Each one of us who received such a letter has cherished it to this day. We were her greatest cheering squad and support system. She regained that skill entirely, until her second stroke episode. So, I say send out the letters and translate where you need to. Don't send them to everyone, but to her dearest ones. It is a treasure to them. Our loved ones need to feel successful at whatever they are doing. These are times when failure seems to be what they are doing a lot of. So we need to be conscious of reinforcing even the littlest successes.

Her joy is now wrapped up in much simpler achievements than her in her past. It's amazing what you cheer for! It's the basic things that make you happy now. And they make her happy also. Reinforcing her in the simple things when she has successfully performed them is a very big deal. A good bowel movement!

She needs to be encouraged. We all need it. Pour it on whenever she does anything good, or half good. It works wonders. It strengthens her. She'll try her hardest to please you, if you are visibly delighted with her efforts.

Smiles work wonders. Genuine smiles always melt the coldest troubles.

Keep It Simple

I keep in mind, now, that her mind can no longer sort out busyness. It's too confusing. So, here is another new aim: Keep things *simple* - simple choices, simple tasks, simple games, simple directions. Don't send her off with three things to do! Simple is the operative word. Keep it simple! If you are too complicated, you set her up for failure. Anxiety reigns high. When we have company, if there are too many people, or she has been at it for hours, she will bail out. Over-stimulation causes withdrawal. It's too confusing trying to sort out all the conversations and cross-talk. She needs peace. Mother used to be at the center of it all! Now, it takes too much out of her to try to keep it all together. Her mind is simple. It's OK to take her into another room, like a den, or bedroom, and let her sit quietly by herself, watching a favorite TV channel. She is happy with the break from the noise and confusion. *I* can enjoy the company, and *she* can enjoy the break from it.

3. Personal Care

Her Body

Little by little you will be the one to have full view of her whole body. You will be the one in a position to note changes, problems, skin abnormalities, any superficial, clear-to-the-eye conditions. You knew every mole, shadow, and birthmark on your baby. You will now know every one on your mother. You are the ever-watchful eyes. One wonderful gift to her is rubbing her down with body lotion, whichever one you think is best. Make her feel wonderful! Her skin now needs it, and it is a treat beyond words, a delicious indulgence! It is in that lovely process of renewing her skin that you see such tender gratitude on her part, and realize a feeling of such tender giving on yours. I'm sure that when she kissed the bottoms of your baby feet on the changing table, you were tickled beyond expression. Your little heart received the love. Hers does too!

The skin of the elderly is particularly dry, and in some places breaks down easily. So, be generous and lather her up with the best lotion you know for moistening skin. Get it in every fold of flesh, places that will chafe, especially if she wears protective undergarments. It will keep her from itching – especially where she can't scratch! The simple things that we take for granted, they have to endure! Mother no longer walks without shoes or slippers, but when she did, we never put lotion between her toes or on the bottoms of her feet – one less opportunity to slip! It's while I am rubbing her with lotion that I take the opportunity to review every square inch of her flesh!

Privacy

You are both sensitive. Your flesh is sacred. So is hers. As you will gradually see more and more of her body, remember: she has entrusted her privacy to you, no one else. Others are not privileged to share her sweet and private space. I remember saying, "Mother, only *you* know whether you are dry or not! I can't feel underneath you!" Well, little did I know that I would be the one to know soon enough! The good news is that rarely does anything change overnight. It usually happens slowly, over time. We are given time to adjust to each difficult change. As I mentioned, there are some things you said you would never do, but - Bingo! You are doing them and willingly, maybe not in the beginning, but soon enough. You are getting better at "taking things as they come."

Bathing

Bathing can be another big challenge. *Safety* is the key word here! I have put grab bars in front and on both sides of her tub. She can get in with minimal assistance (but I never take my hands off her), and she sits on a chair. Then the fun begins, typical childish resistance! But, she really wants that bath. She might resist getting in, but she generally loves it once she's there! She used to help to bathe herself, but now, like so many other things, I do it all. It's just easier and, naturally like a mother, I'm more thorough! We do this once a week. That seems to be quite adequate for her. In fact, when bath night comes, I say, "OK, we're going to get a bath." She'll often reply, "Again? I never take a bath that often." She's serious. I laugh, and we get on with the journey into the tub.

Clothes and Dressing

In the morning, I need all the time I can get, and then some. So, whatever she will be wearing in the morning, I set out the night before. I do whatever I can the night before in order to save steps when I need them most.

Clothes need to be comfortable and easy to get on and off, to lift up or pull down - velcro, not laces; elastic waistbands, not belts! She also needs to be warm. I can tell if she's warm by just taking her hand. If it's cold, she's cold, no matter what the weather! Keep her warm. Her skin is thin. She can catch cold easily.

Remember that clothes are nice. She likes them too, *still!* So treat her. Don't dress her so practically that she looks like she's on her way to the ball game in November or ready to wash the kitchen floor. I try to find practical clothes that look good, nice colors, interesting patterns. It takes a look or two in the stores. But, for the most part, I have been able to find appropriate dresses for my mother. That is what she wears. And many are zip-up-the-front dresses – great to get on and off.

Aside from your favorite outlets, there are organizations which specialize in quality clothing for just this life style. Most can be found through a search on the internet.

Let her wear the things she likes, if she still chooses. Special jewelry - it may be junk to you, but if it has sentimental value to her, by all means, she should wear it.

Looking good makes her feel good. So I tell her how pretty she looks. What a lift!

Toileting

It is this chore that is one of the last you take over. Even if you are in the care-giving business, it is not easy to do this for your mother or your spouse! Slowly but surely, you find that assuming such tasks takes less emotional effort. Cleanliness is very important here. But so is her sensitive skin. It is good, if you can afford it, to use adult, throw-away washcloths. They are very soft and easy on her. For years we have had a high rise toilet seat. She can get up so much more easily from the elevated position. I encourage her to help herself as much as possible. It is good for her, and very good for me! There is a huge difference between minimum assistance and maximum assistance. If she can help you help her getting around and maneuvering, you are way ahead in the game.

Also, give away the fancy bathroom rugs, if they are *not* non-slip. That's a hazard no one can afford!

In the morning, I set a commode beside her bed, so she doesn't have to walk all the way into the bathroom. It saves time and energy. That's one less frustration to start off my day.

As a sweet treat, every morning, while she is sitting on the commode, I wash her back with a nice warm cloth. It feels so good, and she says so, always with such gratitude.

On with the protective underwear! She wears it 24/7. She doesn't always need it, but *I* do! I don't want to be caught short - ever. So it's better, in bed and out, to be protected.

Standing and Walking

If standing is an issue, don't turn your back on her for one minute. You must always be alert, and ready assuming that, resembling a toddler she will likely fall. When I am walking with her, I make her look up. It helps her to walk without tripping over her own feet. Even when she uses a walker, I or whoever is helping her, encourage her to stand and walk erect. It's a constant reminder, as her natural inclination is to bend over like a monkey. She can't balance well, if at all, in that position.

When we were still learning to stand and walk, after her second stroke, transferring from one seat to another was an important chore. Therapists carefully trained both of us in the maneuver. I learned the proper method of lifting from under her arms, balancing her weight, and transferring her to the car, to the potty, etc. It is a time when engaging her at her level of ability is key. Initially she couldn't help me, and I didn't know how to engage her, or determine what she was capable of doing. So we simply grew together. Now, with constant exercise, she is greatly strengthened. I make her place her feet properly under her, and give her the responsibility to help me, encourage her to stand and balance, then, together, we share the "load," and I don't have to carry her whole weight. It's a big help to both of us, but especially me! She's strong and able, and we walk everywhere in our home, with hands together. But, an interesting phenomenon can happen. If I begin bearing her whole weight, she reverts right back to letting me carry it all. So, when family or others offer to help, I show them how to "engage" her.

Food and Feeding

This is a challenge of a different sort. I just remind myself that I don't have to be Julia Child. Whatever I have for dinner is the best for everyone. Of course, that assumes that there is no pre-existing condition which dictates a different diet. An interesting phenomenon began to occur. Mother was always a good eater. She still has her teeth – at ninety-five. And I don't mean two on the bottom and two on the top! She has her teeth, and we brush them, most of the time happily, every day. But again, another change – now she doesn't like to chew. Or, she may well forget, from day to day, how to chew! So, little by little, I have been softening her food, until now I puree it all. Well, the good news is that, if I puree it all, she can eat whatever we eat. I can puree everything early in the week, put it in the refrigerator, and haul it out whenever it's dinner time, warm it up in the microwave, and, presto, dinner within five minutes! That's the best part. It fits my schedule and pace. She eats it without a tussle, and we are all at peace. Peace is everything!

Morning is my favorite time of day. So, keeping it filled with more peace and less stress is the goal. Thus, as I have already said, I set out all the things I need for the morning the night before. I put the breakfast tray out on the kitchen counter. Pills are out, ready to crush. Glasses are out, ready to fill. Plates, silverware, napkins, everything is ready to go. I retire at night as ready for the morning as I can be, with extra minutes in bed, instead of dashing around putting things together while I begin to fall apart.

When she was still able and trustworthy to be home alone, and therefore get her own food out of the refrigerator, I marked it well with clear labels, and left simple instructions in the kitchen on the counter in an obvious place.

One big word of advice: *Take time.* Eating needs to be at a slow and peaceful pace. It most often is not in our current life style. We eat and run, literally. I am most guilty! That needs to change. It has a real affect on their cooperation and ability to respond healthfully, to say nothing of aggravating swallowing issues. Otherwise, this will be one of the most frustrating experiences in all your caregiving. I remember one day when Mother was confused about what she should eat next. I was still in a bit of denial - that she couldn't understand the simple task of picking up the spoon and eating what was in front of her until everything was gone! But it does go that way. I said to her on several occasions, "Mother, I'm *not* going to feed you." I sure ate those words!

Small bites! I tend to shovel it in. Open wide, here comes the spoonful! They can't swallow like a beer drinker anymore. When she fed herself, the chances were that she would not feed herself too much at a time. But, if that were a problem, using a toddler spoon and fork is a good way to limit the size of the mouthfuls.

For the elderly, taste buds grow dim, too. That means that sweet things can be made sweeter and spicy things made spicier, depending on dietary restrictions.

Another interesting phenomenon has to do with the temperature of food. No longer does the temperature of the food have the same appeal. Hot coffee, cold ice cream, cold juice – I even put her ice cream in the microwave, so it is melted on top of the warm cake. Everything is better at room temperature. Everything goes down better if it's room temperature. Boring, but true! And the goal is to get it down. Eating is everything. So, making it tasty, fun and attractive really helps to reach this goal.

Now that I feed her, rejecting food presents another interesting challenge. Why does she do it? It's probably pretty simple. She either is not hungry, doesn't like it, or the spoonfuls are too big. There are many different methods of dealing with it. After you figure out what it may be, then you try to fix it, if you can. But if you can't, and she needs to eat, welcome back to the club of cajolers. Sweet talk, humor, logic, firmness, serious talk! I make conversation to distract her from her predicament. Just as it is with children, one way is not always going to work. This is a real test of patience and creativity. Some people are better at it than others. Some days I'm better at it than on other days. But, always I have my actions underscored and inspired by love, always love.

Of course, some of these phenomena may not fit your mold. You may have others. There will surely be things that you will observe in your loved one that no one else may recognize, but you do. You know her better than anyone, including her physician. Remember, you are in uncharted waters, at least as far as your loved one is concerned.

4. A Day in the Caregiver's Life

———⟡———

A key understanding is that in many matters regarding your loved one, you know more than anyone. Although you are not a physician or a healthcare professional, you are in touch with the "science" of caring for a human being. In that capacity you provide valuable input into the total effort of her care. And if your physician is wise, your advice and observations of physical and mental changes play a major role in any decisions about her care.

Feelings are not Facts!

It doesn't matter how you feel. Your love is demonstrated by your actions. Your love *is* your action. There's frustration – "Sorry I said it!" That's so normal. I just remember – the love is the doing. I try not to compare myself to anyone else. Everyone is different and everyone has different shortcomings. Love overcomes them all. It is love that motivates you to do what you are doing. It is a titanic job. Comparing oneself to others is always a temptation, and perhaps, even a ghost of the family past. It is an evil, sticking up its ugly head. You have to recognize it and deliberately put it aside. Just get busy. That's love. That's what she needs, and so do you.

There's consolation – *Everyone* takes these care-giving steps reluctantly. The overwhelming senses of guilt and abandonment haunt you. You may not be able to put your finger on your exact feelings, but you are just at loose ends, feeling like you want to burst into tears. You're just not ready for this. That's how you feel. It's OK. Hugs work miracles, not words.

Saving Time/Being Organized

Time is our most precious commodity. It doesn't belong to us, and it gets away in a flash. I can't seem to get enough things done with the time I have. I never find enough to do what I want. And, I certainly don't feel that I get enough time to rest from my labors. So, I do as much as I can to save it.

If there is something that takes two hands, I do the two-hand part before I begin the task. For instance, if I have to squeeze ointment from a tube, I squeeze it from the tube and put the dab of ointment on the outside of the tube, so I can get it with one swipe of a free finger, while I'm holding mother with the other hand!

I put ointments and salves always within arm's reach of wherever I need them. Often in more than one place, like bathroom *and* bedroom, so I don't have to stop my stride to get them. *Convenience is everything.*

I even put her overcoat out on her wheel chair, ready for action in the morning. Poor Mother! Getting on her coat, and sitting in her chair, ready to leave, is sometimes a drill. Stand up straight! Right arm; left arm; Turn to the chair. Don't sit down! Stand up straight! Take the right arm of the chair; take the left arm; *now* sit. Finally we're ready to leave for the day. Now we need a rest!

I repeat my time savers: I set out clothes the night before, including underwear. I set up for breakfast the night before. I set up for dinners early in the week, like Sunday night.

Fears

Tenseness is a sign of fear, fear of not understanding what's going on. There are many indefinable fears. The first time I realized that Mother was tense, I worried about whether I had somehow caused her to be "up tight". Maybe my own personality played a role in her not feeling adequate or just unsure about whether she was doing something right. That's a legitimate question. At least for me it was. Was I asking too much of her, or in a way that made me appear to be judging her performance? As it turns out, even though such concern is good, it is not uncommon for the elderly to feel generally afraid. Feeling safe is not so easy when you are little by little giving up control, usually unwillingly, of all that you have held as your right all your life. Your mind plays tricks on you. You don't remember basic things, and you *know* that you don't remember. It simply makes you unsure of yourself and often unsure about what you should be doing next. Uncertainty is frightening. Surrender is frightening. And all the while *we* think that they should have *nothing* to worry about, because we are taking care of *everything!*

I try, again, to use her will to get her to relax. Her fears, which are unconscious for the most part, are what make her rigid. However, her *will* helps to keep her that way. If I catch her on an off moment, I can prove it to myself. She is not stiff all the time. So, if she's not, she can will to relax. You need to help. I tell mother, lovingly, "Let go, relax." I pick up her arm and let it drop until it is free, and she feels relaxed. Stiffness is an ongoing issue. Since it stems from fear, it requires ongoing, tender encouragement to help her let go.

Strange Things that Just Happen

I came home from work one day, and mother was totally at sevens. Completely discombobulated! She couldn't remember where I was, yet this was a typical, normal work day for me. She was in a panic, a state in which I had never seen her before. Although some rather immediate things were evident, I honestly didn't know what was happening. She had wet herself, she, a seven day camel! So, I pulled myself together, and her, cleaned her up and went on to get our dinner. As our habit is to read the Bible and say prayers after dinner, we began to do that. Then I noticed her head turned slightly to the right, as if she were reading out of the left eye. And so she was. She was actually reading out of the left side of both eyes because she indeed had had a mild stroke, which I had not yet discovered. It had affected the right side of both eyes. So she was reading from the left side of both eyes. She had what is termed a "field cut". A section of vision is "cut" out, so you are looking at incomplete information, and trying to piece it together. It's like looking at the world through a Kaleidoscope.

In my limited understanding, I decided that she must have had a stroke. One physician's visit and an MRI proved that to have been so. This was an irreversible event which we would need to add to our list of things that would re-define our lives, especially hers – a writer and a reader! From then on, she would have to live "piecing things together". She would no longer read sensibly without help, or write legibly! And sadly, but clearly, no more piano, the gift was gone.

So now, enter another phenomenon – shut eyes while eating or talking! Is she just resting from the wearisome task of constantly figuring out what she is looking at? Or is she really dozing? It is possible that she is simply resting her eyes while she is carrying on eating, talking, etc. But, it is important to know the difference between just shutting her eyes while still alert, and dozing off in the middle of the moment. It would not be good to be dozing off in the middle of eating. She could choke on her food. So, I engage her. I say, "Mother, open your eyes." This goes on, usually, throughout the meal. It's just part of her routine behavior. I take it as it comes!

Incontinence is another care. It can change with varying circumstances. Mother's two strokes caused incontinence. But, after some time, in each case, it cleared up. This is a condition that comes and goes. I now carry with me at all times my "supplies" bag – briefs, ointment, gloves, wash cloth. And, at night, we take no chances. She sleeps with protective underwear and a bed pad underneath. We are doubly protected and at peace. We sleep well.

Changes in behavior can signal some "event", such as a TIA, which is really a mini stroke, in laymen's terms. These events can happen in her sleep. They can happen before your eyes. Whenever Mother suffers from unexplained restlessness, long bouts of confusion, or mood swings, I consider the real possibility of her having endured another event.

Humor

You may feel as if the walls are caving in sometimes. But the best medicine is a sense of humor. We must see the light side. I try to take myself lightly, especially my feelings and priorities. "That's easier said than done," you say. I couldn't agree more. Nonetheless, I try, and keep trying. Often after a particularly challenging episode is over, and I am exhausted, I repeat it to another person, with some humor. It's absolutely healing! We need this levity. It colors everything "good".

Laugh a lot. We remember fun things in our past, silly incidents, funny stories, good jokes. We repeat the punch lines and laugh, laugh, laugh. Reader's Digest is right. "Laughter is the Best Medicine" - for you and your loved one. You'll laugh and you'll hug. Especially laugh at *your* mistakes, *not* hers. If you laugh at her mistakes, it may appear that you are laughing at her, and that is a bad thing. Embrace hers, and laugh at yours. While she's laughing, she's apt to do the very thing that you have been trying unsuccessfully to get her to do.

Pets Are Important!

Pets Always Bring a Smile

Caregiver, Callie "signs in" with Sebastian and Benni Beau

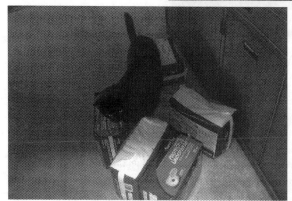

Packing up the Pull-ups

Pets

Both children and adults are generally favorably affected by the presence pets. They seem to bring a sense of warmth, security and serenity. Petting them, loving them, being with them brings sweet peace and joy. They also seem to provide unexpected, delightful entertainment. One day, one of our cats, Sebastian, was watching Benni Beau, the bird, take a bath in his water dish. The cat, who likes to drink from the bird's cup, was only a wing's length away from the bathing bird. He was waiting patiently for the bird to finish bathing, so he could get his drink. All the while the bird was taking his time, watching the cat watch him bathe. This tease of a bird was totally in charge, and we were all doubled up in laughter – Mother Love, Callie, our caregiver, and I. These kinds of episodes lighten our evenings often. A pet is a creature that doesn't need verbal communication to receive our love. No matter what our mood or thinking, we simply can be in each other's company, feeling loved.

What's interesting is that stuffed animals bring Mother great comfort and fun also. My sister recently gave her an owl, which she promptly named WOO (Wise Old Owl). She held the creature lovingly, admiring his bright and all-knowing eyes. Then, from her wealth of childhood treasures, in her classic, all-knowing teacher look, she recited a familiar rhyme:

A wise old owl sat in an oak.
The more he saw, the less he spoke.
The less he spoke, the more he heard.
We should all be like that wise old bird!

Proud and happy, she lovingly held the feathery, stuffed creature. A sweet moment! We enjoy many of them.

Thankfulness

I am genuinely thankful. I have lots of reasons to be. So, I work at counting those reasons every day, especially when I'm feeling a little stressed or weary. Most often they turn my frown into a smile. I need the gratitude. It leads to more gratitude, then joy, and then a sweet sense of how loved I am. All the trials are dimmed by the over-arching sweet savor of goodness that emanates from a thankful heart. If you find that your loved one is not very thankful, you start it! It will catch on. It cannot be helped. Thankfulness begets thankfulness.

Sweetness should be a regular part of the menu. You may say, "*My* mother never was sweet!!" Try it. The toughest respond. It's contagious. You start the "thank you", "I'm sorry", "please" and "excuse me". You do the little courtesies and she *will* respond.

If she never had it before in life, it will be the dawn of a new day – for both of you. It dissolves the negative air!

Pray

A Creator who loves you and takes care of you both is there every minute waiting for you to give a glance and ask for help. Even when you forget, you are bolstered up beyond your wildest imagination. But, oh how surprised you will be when out of nowhere you give a nod for help or a simple thank you. The response will be pressed down and running over – just when you need it. I find most often that I get all the help I need.

Generations Pray together

Prayer is the Staple of Life for Mother Love

David and Family Join in Prayer

For all the things Mother forgets, her prayers are not included. She remembers every prayer, and only needs an occasional word to recall those deeply seated treasures. When in a tizzy or off the track, just reciting a prayer brings her back. Nothing has as profound an influence on her spirit as her prayers.

Participating in the religious services of our Faith has been a regular part of our routine, all our life long. So now nothing has changed. I take her faithfully as long as she can get up. It is a true source of peace and love, consolation and strength. Nothing is better for her spirits, or mine for that matter, than this lift. In the face of almost constant change, this is an unchanging constant!

Sleep

You can't get too much sleep, you or your loved one! Your body *and* mind need a big break. So, make up your mind. Treat yourself and her to lots of sleep. Twelve hours a night is not too much for the elderly. Then, when you get her up in the morning, she is fresher, more alert, and has more energy to do the things you want her to do in the day. If you have concerns about her getting out of bed at night, a bed rail works wonders. It's just enough to keep her in, and not enough to close her in. It will give both you and her peace. You won't be wondering in the night whether she's fallen out of bed! If I awaken, I check up on her. Sometimes I refresh her pillows and covers, as she occasionally shifts uncomfortably through the night.

Another real boon is the baby monitor. With one beside her bed and one beside mine, I can get a good night's sleep. Now I am sensitive to her every sound, yet sleep through the unimportant noises. If you ever used this with a child, you know how it works.

In fact sometimes she rattles on like a little child in a crib. I don't try to discern her conversation. I'm just glad she's content. In those situations I occasionally turn down the volume, so I can ignore her!

Getting her to bed early gives me the quiet time in the evening. I grab this sweet, though brief moment. I need it. Just to relax and have a few minutes of peace before I plan tomorrow. Or, I plan tomorrow, and then take the break. Oh how good a few minutes' peace feels. It rejuvenates me, mentally, emotionally and physically.

I recommend taking breaks throughout the day. That doesn't necessarily mean "naps". It just means quiet time. Slow down, "veg out". When we were in grammar school, it used to be graham crackers and milk, and "put your head down on your desk" for 10 minutes. Same story, different millennium!

Goodnight

At the end of the day, usually long and often tiring, just remember, you know your loved one better than anyone, better than the physician, better than your siblings. You see her all the time. So, don't be surprised if you see phenomena which the physician can't really explain. You are on new turf in the world of living. The elderly are presenting new conditions everyday to the medical community. You are often swimming in uncharted waters. Therefore, your senses are as important, or more so, as anyone's. Others who see her on a daily basis should check in with you about what they have seen in a day that may be different from the day before, or different from their experience of your mother. Sleep well.

5. Relationships

It is often said that you reverse your roles. You are now the parent, and your mother is now the child. Well, that is not altogether true. The only thing that reverses is the care- giving. But the relationship will always be that you are the child and your parent is the parent. The sanctity of that relationship will not only be kept in tact but, because of it, you will grow in ways you cannot measure - such as your respect for your mother, the unspoken acknowledgement of her position in the hierarchy of life, the wisdom that she has that you don't have yet (you haven't been there), countless ways in which you cannot turn the tables, and they will not be turned for you either, if you are someday in the same place. Both you and she know that she has been more places in life than you have, maybe not physically, but emotionally and practically. It borders on true reverence on your part, as you watch her let go of all that she once had, and lay it down, accepting the new station in life. This is a new relationship. Nothing has ever been like it for you. And, if you are someday on the other end, you will still be in a different relationship. You were never there before.

Sibling or Family Responsibility

What about the family? This is a touchy subject. And, folks outside the family, meaning well, will often ask if other siblings are doing their share. But, other siblings may not have the time, proximity, or resources – mental, emotional or physical - to take on a commitment of this proportion. Whatever the reason may be, your personal response to the need has put you where you are. If brothers and sisters are of the same mind as you, they will come forth. Above all, you don't want to put your family members under *your* gun, suffering guilt placed on them by you. Even if you think you are being fair, you are not if you lay a silent burden on them to which they don't honestly feel they can respond. The total family needs to feel together in support of each other in this big job.

Everyone has a role to play in the health of the family and its dynamic. By far and away yours is the biggest role, but the rest of the family are your vital support and life-line. You need their love. Make sure you thank them for all that they give. They need to feel tied into your life. It is their mother, too. And, in a way, you are sharing things with your mother that they cannot – special moments, deep sentiments, profound truths, secret feelings and vulnerabilities. It's a treasure without measure.

Although not everyone in the family feels the call to take on elder care, everyone has an opinion about the care. My brother-in-law likes to tell his children, "If there are two people in a room, there will be a difference of opinion!"

Family stress is inevitable in this care-giving world. Even in the closest families, and ours is one of the closest I know, there are individual hot buttons with which to contend especially when the loved one is a parent. We all have differing perspectives. It is hard to listen. It's as if the family dynamic of our childhood is back again! We need to look at loving and overlooking. It's truly a time of great stress. It is good to remember that everyone has the same goal – the best for Mother. Health care professionals are a solid source of strength and balance. You don't need to carry important decisions as if they were your own. Family meetings with the professionals are healthy and helpful. They can be the best antidote for family differences. When Mother had her shoulder replacement, three of us, my sister, a brother, and I, along with Mother, met with the physician. His explanations and manner were most assuring, and we all left the consultation on the same page, having heard the same things. It was indeed settling.

Lastly, you can never over-communicate. Keeping everyone in the loop goes a very long way in making everyone comfortable with the day-to-day decisions. Remember, everyone has the same goal. But the primary caregiver should have the final say. This is a critical family dynamic. You should be trusted by your siblings to make wise decisions, which they don't need to question.

Quality Time

Family members who live nearby have occasions to be with Mother rather often and in many different circumstances. As such, they have the chance to see her and share with her for extended periods of time. They get to see her at her best and at her worst. They have more opportunities to experience "special moments" that cannot be planned, but only happen spontaneously.

However, family members who live far away should try their best to make blocks of time to be with their parent. It's not a simple one-hour visit, and the obligation met! (It should hardly

Quality Time With the Family

Thanksgiving With
Every Generation

The Two Sisters,
90 & 95, Enjoy a
Hearty Laugh

Son, Andrew and wife,
Mary Ann Share a
Little Sing Along

Everyone is Family
to Mother Love

be thought of as an "obligation"!) Quality time is important not only for the parent, but for the family member. Spontaneity doesn't happen on command. You have to be around one another to expect spontaneous and memorable things to "happen". So vacations should have their fair share of "time with Mother." The investment reaps dividends of non-repeatable loving keepsakes. And everyone needs to experience the parent's current status – all that it is now.

The Advocate

There is *one primary advocate – YOU*! You may occasionally step on someone's toes. It just happens. This is *not* license. You have a weighty responsibility to keep this individual, just as you would your child. In many ways that is what she is. We're not rude, just swift and sure. Apologize when necessary and go on. *Apologize!!!!!* There is no more important word than apologize, except Love! Love automatically makes apologizing easier. It means being able to say you're sorry when you don't even think you are wrong. It means saying you're sorry when you are too ashamed to say so. It means saying you're sorry whenever the moment seems to beckon for that precious ointment of humility.

To maintain any regular pace seems like an overwhelming task. Some people can do it better than others. Some days are better than others. Outside resources can really do a great job in bringing sanity and freedom to your life, and peace and joy to your loved one's life. Those opportunities are explored next.

Mardi Gras – Gala Time With the Advocate

Mother Love and the Advocate

6. Resources

I'll never forget the mysterious pamphlet on Elder Care that showed up on Mother's bedside table, when she was in recovery from her near-fatal burn accident. I was shocked and angry. I was shocked because that communication should have come more gently and in person. I was angry because I didn't want my mother, who had most of her wits about her at that point, to see what was being suggested. She wouldn't be ready for that news, *and I certainly wasn't.* My denial was not clear to me at that point. I really felt strongly about the issue. I honestly had not yet assessed her level of independence.

However, when you finally decide that it is unhealthy for her to stay at home alone, and you can't keep arranging to take her places, or to have people "stop by" which wears out for even the best of us, then you must look at your options for her daily care. You can either arrange for her to stay at home with in-house coverage, or seek an outside, daytime activity center, at her level of participation.

For all practical purposes, there are three kinds of need that take you into various directions for support: Financial, physical and circumstantial. They affect the level of support you seek and what you can expect to receive. Where do you begin? Any of the following provide good direction:

A. County Department of Aging and Adult Services

Your County Department of the Aging is one of the first places to go. They can tell you the laws, what is available and how you apply for assistance.

B. State Department of the Aging

In my home state of Pennsylvania, the Department of the Aging publishes *A Guide for Family Caregivers of Older Pennsylvanians*. This guide neatly provides helpful tips on just about every concern, and how to start addressing your own concerns. Every state will have similar resources.

C. Federal Health Organizations

In Washington, DC, the Council on Family Health, produces simple, easy-to-understand tips on many levels of concern, such as, *Medicines and You: a Guide for Older Americans*. This is just one of many pamphlets which come out of that organization.

D. Doctors' offices

Ask your physician. There are usually plenty of pamphlets in the waiting area of the doctor's office from various Health Care Providers and Pharmaceuticals.

E. Your own Health Maintenance Organization

The Social Services Department, in your own Health System, can point you to resources in your area, their availability, rules and requirements. They often have their own.

F. Private Institutions

There are private organizations which conveniently package the concerns of aging adults and dispense them throughout the community, as well as through religious organizations.

G. Case Management Services

These organizations specialize in doing the legwork you would ordinarily do in finding the proper resources to fit your need.

H. Religious Institutions

Always consider your religious leaders. They are involved in the community and have many contacts. They also know *you*, and know your circumstances. They can direct you and support you in love.

There could be many other resources in your community. Even the local library may be a viable resource. It can be a frustrating and wearisome task, but at the other end there are answers and there is comfort.

The highly reviewed book, *The 36 Hour Day*, by Nancy Mace and Peter Rabins, is packed with volumes of helpful advice. It is worth reading, and keeping handy as a sort of guidebook. In its section called, "Locating Resources" it says, " You will need to be persistent and may need to contact several individuals or agencies. The process of locating resources can be long and tedious. If you are providing most of the supervision and care of an impaired person, you may feel too overwhelmed to do this." My sister, in fact, made the initial calls that opened the door to help. Check all Resource Guides. Ask anyone in the caregiving community. If nothing else, they can always point you in some direction that is a part of your networking solution.

The first thing we did was pick up the phone book, and look under *Government Listings*. One call led to another, until I found the help I needed. Almost everyone I spoke to was very helpful, indeed, and sympathized with my emotional frailty as well as my circumstances.

Basically, it is best to choose the organizations which are local to you and your community. They know what they can do for you, and they know how to point you in the most appropriate direction, or at least the beginning steps of the long journey to proper care, given your situation.

Financial burdens are very real for many of us. It is appropriate to determine if your loved one qualifies for financial help. There are many approaches to payment plans, sharing the cost, and in-home plans. It is always best if you can keep your loved one in your home with you and use the community resources that support that choice. Everyone is happier. She remains more functional, longer. And, it is cheaper for everyone – you and the state!

Some services, like Senior Centers in the community, are provided by tax dollars and are open to everyone at no extra cost. But other facilities do have a cost, where financial considerations may be a burden.

Let's look at some of the care facilities.

Senior Centers – Your loved one has to be relatively independent about eating, walking, and toileting, to be able to take advantage of these centers. There are generally programs, educational seminars about topics that are meaningful to seniors, such as wills, nutrition, health tips, and world events. Often regular day trips are planned. Some centers even have computer courses! This is all about keeping them engaged *meaningfully*. We're not "putting them" somewhere, while we get on with our lives! They have been around the world – or at least the barnyard – and still have much to give and share. Certainly that is true for my mother. And so the community Senior Center was a good solution for some years, providing constructive things for her to do. Whatever the activity, it is a blessing – for her *and* me.

Adult Day Care – This is care for those who need more supervision. The staffs at these facilities are saints! They absolutely are called to the task. They meet each client at the point of need and engage her at her personal level. Activities are professionally planned to reach all levels of participation. More able participants help out in ways that give them a sense of accomplishment and purpose. These centers can do more for your loved one than you can! *And,* it gives you the very much-needed help you may not even think you are looking for. You can't do it alone. You need the physical *and* emotional support. You need the break in the day.

Just remember, no one takes a loved one to a Day Care Facility *willingly*! This is a last resort, not a first one. Reluctance is the best description of most people's feelings about bringing a loved one to a day care. Even the word "Day Care" doesn't feel good. So, at best the caregiver is reluctant to leave "Mother" there. You feel you are somehow giving up. A rush of guilt just rises up at the level of your neck, literally making you sick. How could you abandon her? She's not "that bad". Maybe something else can be worked out. And on and on it goes! There *is* a certain stigma associated with taking advantage of these services. Fear and guilt take an unmerciful front row seat in your heart. But just remember, feelings are not facts! Love is action. So, if all goes well, slowly but surely, everyone gets acquainted. The caregivers in the center get to know you and your mother. You get to know them. You do become "family". It fortunately just happens. The defenses come down. Your look of dismay turns to a smile of gratitude. The gates to each other's hearts are open.

An important caveat! Not all centers are created equal. In the main, they are. However, just like any other service, you need to

Resources – Warm, Loving, and Caring

Great Nephew Shares
a Tender Moment

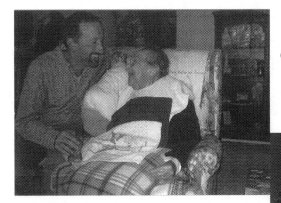

Love Abides Between Callie
and Mother Love

The Day Center – A
Hub of Activity for
Everyone

Bonding Happens
at the Center

check them out. I went with mother to visit the Adult Day Center in our community, twice before the day we started. We saw the center in action. We were tentative, but they were relaxed, real, and delightfully warm. It was a "go", even though we (or at least, I) were still wary at that moment. After mixing for a little while, you can tell if a place is healthy. People are who they are, no matter who is around. If inappropriate behavior or language is tolerated at home, it is sure to show up in a place such as the Day Care, where people are simply who they are, no more pretenses or front covers. Watch for behavior or language that you may find inappropriate. Indecent exposure or inappropriate behavior is not a right in a public place. If you find yourself uncomfortable, don't expose your loved one to that environment. If it offends you, it will offend her. Remember, she has to be there all day, every day. Will she be "at home"?

Truly the Adult Day Center in our community is a model facility. In a recent fundraising letter, the Center is quoted as, "providing a safe, therapeutic, and respectful environment for frail elderly and disabled adults." That is a modest statement. Situated in a large old house, it gives you a sense of "home" when you first walk in. Pets - two guinea pigs, a host of birds, and a family dog - are an integral part of the daily life. It is so "home" that mother is constantly confused as to where home really is! Structured activities which engage the "participant" at her level of ability are properly balanced throughout carefully planned days. A staff of true professionals, along with volunteers possessing warmth and caring, is committed to the well-being of your loved one and the family. They make it what it is – a healthy, loving home, close to home.

Caregivers – These wonderful professionals come to your home and help with feeding your loved one, personal care, and getting her ready for bed. It's a big deal. Even if you are there, *they* are in charge of the caring for the time they are there. I take full advantage of the break – emotional and physical. I need it!

Our lovely caregiver, who is employed by a home care provider, walked into our home, and with her special gift she just sized up our little world. She took over *her* job responsibilities with sensitivity to who we were, and began to be part of our dynamic. From the minute she arrived, she was carefully assessing who this new client was. She knew her job responsibilities. But she also knew how to size up the new horizon. We have pets - a bird and two cats, a high-strung primary caregiver (me), and a ninety-five-year-old loving and sweet "client", Mother Love. Callie Brown fast became a member of the family. She took charge of the bird quickly, a trick for a Sun Conure. The cats soon considered her a part of the family. So we all have a special time together, when Callie is with us. She does her work. I get my break even when I'm there all the time, and we all laugh more than most. It is a spiritually healthy time, filled with God's love and encouragement. We couldn't live without her. Her picture with the bird is glued to the refrigerator door with all the rest of the family!

Medicare SNF – Skilled Nursing Facility – This is "halfway" or transitional care between a hospital stay and the final trip home. A great idea! Of course, you must always be the advocate overseeing the transition. Are you getting what you think you need? In other words, is the facility offering enough, or can you just as well get it with the combination of resources at your regular disposal in your normal, daily routine? One thing you *don't* want is to have your loved one sitting around staring at walls. Every day she is not "engaged" is a potential setback, mentally and physically. You want her "back in the saddle" as quickly as possible. You are the judge, with helpful advice of course.

Respite – Nursing Home Respite – for *you!* If you need a break you can have your mother stay in a nursing home for perhaps a few days, or a week, giving you the time to go where you need for whatever you need – vacation, work, travel. But check out the facility. This break is available in-house or in a nursing home.

Seeking the right support is one giant step for the caregiver, the loved one, and the family. Understandably, we are so reluctant to take it. My father used to say that we always have three reasons for doing (or not doing, in this case) something: The first reason is the one that sounds good. The second is the one you want others to think is the real reason. The third is the real reason. So, with this care-giving decision, there are three kinds of reasons we give for not proceeding with the help we need:

i. Financial – we don't see how we can do it.
ii. Circumstantial – we have too many obstacles in our daily routine to make something like this work.
iii. Emotional – we're simply not able, or ready, to face it all.

Thus, following my father's formula, the third reason – emotional – is the real reason why we don't do it, usually. I'm suggesting that our emotions are the things that generally stand in our way. We think, "It's wonderful that *you* are taking advantage of that resource. As long as it's happening to *you*, it's OK. But not my Mother!" We must get over the raging guilt – thinking "my mother (husband) is just not that in need." If you get past your feelings, you are poised for a breath of fresh air, not a dark tunnel of abandonment. It's a community thing, a family thing. It takes everyone upholding everyone.

Help!

Accept help! Wherever it comes from, accept it. Family, friends, official resources like senior centers, day care, and the like. We are so reluctant to seek or accept help initially. Yet, it is indeed our saving grace.

7. Keeping Her Well

Physical Healing

E verything is slow to heal. Even things which should take no time at all, or appear to warrant no attention, seem to take forever to get back to normal. Mother had a sore on the side of her tongue which by most standards should have gone away quite naturally within a few days, assuming you use the standard kinds of surface ointments and gargles, and perhaps vitamins. Not so! Two weeks later I was watching it and giving her more B vitamins. Then, not wanting to overdo the B vitamins, I switched to Vitamin C to boost her immune system. That went on for days. Slowly the sore diminished. Was it time, vitamins, good oral care, or some combination? Surely, all played some part. Time probably played the biggest part, and the rest shored it up.

Skin irritations also are irksome things. They seem to "keep coming back". Actually, because mother likes to scratch, which is a never-ending battle, I have decided that her skin issues are directly related to her access to the bothersome area. I now try to keep her nails closely clipped. Wearing gloves is also a major deterrent.

Keeping clean hands and a warm room are probably the two most basic and appropriate things to do.

Hospitals

The effect of hospital stays on the elderly is legendary! No matter how fine your hospital is, it's not home. The elderly need the stability of home. They need the familiar. It is their security. Remember, the mind is so fragile. In the life of the elderly, just changing the surroundings can have a huge affect on their recognition, and therefore their security. When they are home, they are safe. So, while they are in the hospital, be sure to be around them as much as possible. Or, have someone they know and love around them. If you have friends or family close by and available, they perhaps can share the load. It will keep your loved one engaged, in the safety of family and friends.

Whenever I must take mother to the hospital, I also take big wall charts. Actually they have sticky backs to them. I make signs large enough for mother to read from her bed, and put them all over the walls. If she doesn't read them herself, everyone else who comes in the room reads them! They help the staff to reinforce her, and it also serves to communicate with others. They are a help to everyone. Keeping her oriented is the primary concern.

However, you have other reasons for being there. You need to be involved in the care. While you trust the medical staff, and indeed I have not seen any that were not committed to the well-being of their patients, they do make mistakes. Mistakes are just that. We are not here to point fingers, but to get well. Whatever it takes, you are the advocate responsible for the well-being of your mother. She is your #1 responsibility. No matter how good the caregivers in the hospital are, every patient can't be their #1 priority. They do have other patients. Therefore, if nothing else, you are an expeditor. You do your best to follow up on medications.

Make sure you know exactly what she is being given and how much. That will possibly save something from falling through the cracks. Accompany her to tests. You are her security. She is safe when you are by her side, especially when she is waiting her turn for tests. You feed her. You take care of the little attention-giving chores that the already-overworked staff usually has to do. You do them. That's love in action, and it will give the staff a break. They will be grateful. They need your help, too. Every day they face difficulties and difficult people! You can be a light in their life. If there is an extra step that you can take for them (and her), they will surely be grateful.

If your loved one is in the hospital for an extended stay, ask to have a family meeting with your physician. Conferences make a difference in clear communication. Everyone has a chance to hear first hand and speak first hand. Obviously such meetings are not practical on a regular basis unless your loved one is in critical care. But, e-mail communications, or faxes left for the doctor can give the doctor a jump on understanding what your issues are, and what you, as a family, want to know about your loved one's care and condition. The key is, *be involved.*

If there are specialist visits, be there. If there are regular doctor visits, be there. Be sure to be in the loop of communication and opinion. Decisions are often made with *your* input, if you are there. I make it a point to be there as much as possible. It lights up her face, and helps the healing process for us both.

Therapy

Although there are different kinds of therapy for different needs, the most important therapy for mother has been physical therapy.

It's different for others, perhaps. But for her, physical therapy was paramount. Getting up, walking, turning around, transferring from seat to seat, to car, to potty, etc. It is amazing how that alone will make the biggest difference in the level of energy *you* have to expend. You are either carrying her everywhere, or she is helping you. You want her help. And, she feels better if she can give it. It's definitely a two way street. One day out "of the swing", and you could lose two. If at all possible, she needs to keep active every day, even when under the weather. There's no rest from staying in shape.

The Physician

Probably one of your best friends, and *your* strongest advocate, is your physician. This is one of the most important relationships you will ever have. It is worth working on. If you don't trust your physician, get another one! If you *do* trust your physician, show it. As I have said before, your physician doesn't know your mother as well as you do. However, if you have been a patient of his for any length of time, you will realize that his educated response to her needs is as trustworthy as your educated guess is. The advice you get, the real, honest sharing about circumstances and remedies, is very important to your peace of mind, as well as your loved one's better health. There are options. Often, there is more than one way to solve a problem. Between the two of you, the best solution will be found. But, have an attitude up front that accepts his authority, knowledge, and good judgment. If you don't believe it, then bail him out. He's not just a handy reference guide that you crack open when all your own remedies seem to fail. He is your *partner!*

I make it my business to communicate as often as I need to. I send faxes or e-mails. I leave phone messages. He always responds to my queries. I trust him. That's everything. He genuinely cares about mother. That's paramount. When best efforts are made with discernment and genuine concern, I find the quality of care is always tops.

Other Health Care Professionals

Your pharmacist, another one of your partners, also has a wealth of knowledge for you to count on. There are pharmacies that are open twenty four hours a day, so you can get help at 3 AM, and *gladly*, I might add! I was desperate one night recently, at 4AM. It was a true crisis, in what I discerned was my mother's reaction to a medication. For once, in an emergency, I actually had a clear head, and thought, "call the pharmacist!" It was a brilliant idea. The right answer was forthcoming. I had a workable solution within minutes. No 911; no ER; no waiting for a call back, just a quick, good answer. There are people in your day-to-day path who have been trained in some way that may be helpful just at the moment of your need. Such are the folks at Day Care, Visiting Nurse Associations, health aides, family members who are in the Health Care business. The list is long. It is wise to make up an emergency call list, so, when you need it, you don't have to think about it. You just go into action.

Home Remedies

Home remedies are as sacred as politics and religion. You have your own ideas, and everyone who gives you advice seems to have his or her own. You swear by them. They swear by them. Some are crazy. Some are worthless. Some really work. But all are beyond criticism. So this is tricky turf, to say the least. If nothing else, if you trust your physician, you should run your remedy by him, even if that's all you do! You must remember that even if you think you are an expert about your rock solid therapy, the body is an intricately coordinated plant, run by delicately balanced chemicals, fueled by well balanced nutrition which supplies the perfect balance of vitamins, minerals, protein, fats, carbohydrates which your plant needs to operate efficiently. Physicians and others have taken years of education to provide them with a knowledge level that the average person doesn't have, even though there are probably more books on nutrition and healthy living than any other subject in the book store! All experts, of course!

It's All In Her Smile!

8. In the End of Life

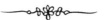

Honesty

The way we view the end of life greatly colors the way we prepare for the inevitable time of our departure from this world. Mother has a very healthy attitude. It is a natural part of her journey, as we believe that life is changed, not ended. This certainly makes our conversing about it and planning for it easier.

Mother may not retain most things, but much of the time she gets it while she is in the midst of it. So I share as much as I can, lovingly, and the best way I know how. I particularly share with her, as appropriate, things about her health. I only omit what would be harmful. And if she asks, I definitely tell her. She is not in the dark. I don't alarm her. I choose carefully and include her, as I plan and communicate about her care. I want her to know that I regard her understanding to be important to her well-being.

End Things

It is critical that everyone in the family has a clear understanding of the "end things" that are important to her. What does she want? How does she want her life here to close? When her departure finally arrives, you want that moment to be as peaceful and loving as possible - for you and her, but especially for you, and her beloved family. You should have a clear plan in place. Know definitively what to do, whom to call. Have it clear. You probably don't want the professionals in emergency care. It is their mission to restore life, not to close it. That is most likely *not* what you want at this point. Your options are your physician, clergy, funeral director. He or she should already be prepared, in your loop.

No matter how simple, write down the plan. Make multiple copies of it. Give it to at least one other member of your family, your funeral director (If you don't have one, get one), your clergy or appropriate final caregiver. Prepay the bills, if you can. This lifts a big burden. All major decisions are made long before they are executed. Get all the paperwork done now! Having the plans behind you is a great relief for *you*. When the hour of departure comes, it will not be filled with unnecessary anxieties, which so often beset us when we are unprepared. Often family dynamics are strangely strained upon the death of a loved one, especially a parent. Having this monumental task well in place relieves much of the unexpected strain.

I learned a great lesson from my aunt, whose departure was so sweet and swift. I was the Executrix of her estate. She had everything in place, all documents and procedures well defined and complete - healthcare directives, living will, Power of Attorney, Will, and all bills prepaid. Everything was in place and clearly available with copies for appropriate people. She wrote to me, sometime before her death, "I want my death, for you, to be like a feather in the wind." It was. I thank her for that regularly, now, and tell others about her example. We are likewise now prepared! Life goes on, allowing us the freedom to live and love a day at a time, without the dying casting a shadow on our horizons.

Love to the Last

It is through caring for Mother that I show her that my love for her is the most important thing I have to give her. All else pales in comparison to that goal. All else is framed by that goal. It defines my life with her. Even through my frustrations, impatience, and mistakes, she *knows* that I love her. Caring for her is the demonstration. It is love in action. My love is my action. Just the other day, Mother sweetly took my hand in both of hers, and kissed it. She said, "The dearest thing you say is when you call me 'Mother Love.'"

Ah yes, if everything is settled the best you know how, your hearts are able to focus on the important things – like remembering how much you love her and she loves you. Then it will almost "just happen" that you "take things as they come."

For today's rapidly growing elder population, tender care, the comforts of home, love, warmth and security, and especially encouragement shape this winding road "home".

In the Sunset of Life Only Love Remains

Afterword

Shortly after this work was finished, at the age of ninety-eight, Mother Love died as sweetly as she lived, surrounded by those who loved and cared for her. Her gracious essence, her love, her joy, her wisdom remain ever present, along with her tender smile.

Shaped by the bedrock, day-to-day experiences of more than ten years of minimum to maximum care for Mother, I continue my outreach daily to the elderly and their families, dipping into this deep well of life, preserving the dignities and sensitivities of our aging loved ones.

Testimonials

—⚬⬦⚬—

"The whole book is very helpful to caregivers because it breaks taboos and talks about decline and death in such an unblinking style. It is bedrock practical and a skin-close intimate look at caregiving to a beloved aging parent by a heroically devoted daughter. It's loaded with little tricks to help the "medicine go down" for both care-ee and care-or".

Charles L. Cooper, PhD, Clinical Psychologist, Director and CEO, Human Resource Consultants, PA, Mental Health Group Practice, central North Carolina

"As a caregiver and a professional in Aging, I found this wonderful book very uplifting. It reinforced all that I knew to be true. I was reminded, when the going gets tough, that the opportunity to do the giving is a treasure."

Ruth Mooney, PhD, MN, Nursing Research Facilitator, ChristianaCare Health System

"The author has portrayed a very personal and realistic life and disease that every child with a living parent should read. She has related in clear, loving terms the life a person with dementia. The recording of her learning experiences, her frustrations, and solutions to problems cannot but help anyone who reads this.

William W. Lander, MD, Family Physician, Past President of the Pennsylvania Medical Society; Fellow – American Academy of Family Physicians

"A lot of **good**, compact information! Great emphasis on the dignity and respect an individual deserves and needs as he or she travels down the path of life and is touched by the aging process."

Stephanie Yocum, B.S Therapeutic Recreation, Certified Dementia Management Specialist, Past Director, MLADC

"As the author breaks her rich experience down into chapters, she identifies key issues in being a caregiver and offers insights that only a caregiver can give."

Kent Bream, MD, University of Pennsylvania, Medical Director, Sayre Health Center

It was my privilege to interview Martha Eischen on our local television station about her book *Mothering Mother.* Everything Martha writes about is rooted in her own experience of caring for her mother for over 10 years. She is very honest about the difficulties and challenges involved in caring for an aging parent. She offers practical approaches to many situations a caregiver faces, and recognizes the importance of addressing the whole person, i.e. their physical, emotional, social, and spiritual needs. Having parents who are in their 90's and are facing some of the aging issues Martha discusses, I learned much from her wisdom. I enthusiastically recommend *Mothering Mother* to anyone who is dealing with issues surrounding the aging process.

The Rev. Michael Pearson, Rector, St. Mary's Episcopal Church, Wayne, PA

"This book has a special meaning because it is written about a very special person's descent into dementia, by a daughter, with unparalleled energy and good will. The book contains a formula for dealing with this illness, plus an excellent guide to resources available."

Hermine Isaak, Member, Lupus Foundation
and past Board Member of the
Southeast Pennsylvania Chapter

"<u>Wonderful</u> job! I am really impressed and grateful for such a kind, sensible, and loving work."

**Dorianne N. O'Hara, R.N. (Retired),
Critical Care Clinician**